SEA TORTOISE

A Comprehensive Guide To Sea Tortoises' Evolution, Ecology, Anatomy, Behavior, Cultural Significance, Lifecycles, History, Species, Feeding, And Conservation In Marine Ecosystems

Ethan Harry

Table of Contents

CHAPTER ONE

INTRODUCTION TO SEA TORTOISES

Overview Of Sea Tortoises

Sea tortoises, commonly known as sea turtles, are fascinating and majestic creatures that have roamed the world's oceans for millions of years. As large, ocean-dwelling reptiles, they possess unique adaptations that allow them to thrive in marine environments. Unlike their land-dwelling relatives, sea tortoises have streamlined bodies and flippers instead of legs, enabling them to glide gracefully through the water with minimal effort. These adaptations are essential for their survival, as they navigate vast oceanic distances throughout their lives.

There are seven recognized species of sea tortoises, each with distinct characteristics and habitats. These species include the leatherback, green, hawksbill, loggerhead, Kemp's ridley, olive ridley, and the flatback turtle. They can be found in all of the world's oceans, from the warm tropical waters to the temperate zones. However, they are notably absent from the coldest waters of the polar regions, where the harsh conditions are unsuitable for their survival.

Sea tortoises are known for their impressive migratory patterns. Many species undertake long-distance migrations between feeding grounds and nesting sites. For instance, the leatherback turtle, the largest of all sea turtles, can travel thousands of miles across the ocean. These migrations are driven by the need to find suitable habitats for feeding and reproduction. Sea tortoises feed on a variety of marine life, including jellyfish, seaweed, crustaceans, and algae. Their diet varies depending on the species and their age, with some being more specialized in their feeding habits.

One of the most remarkable aspects of sea tortoise behavior is their nesting process. Female sea tortoises return to the beaches where they were born to lay their eggs, a phenomenon known as natal homing. They crawl ashore, dig nests in the sand, and deposit dozens to hundreds of eggs. After covering the nests with sand, they return to the sea, leaving the eggs to incubate under the sun's warmth. After several weeks, the hatchlings emerge and make their perilous journey to the ocean, guided by the natural light reflecting off the water's surface.

Despite their resilience and adaptability, sea tortoises face numerous threats, many of which are human-induced. Habitat destruction, pollution, climate change, and illegal poaching for their shells, meat, and eggs have significantly impacted sea tortoise populations. Conservation efforts are crucial to their survival, involving international cooperation, habitat protection, and public awareness campaigns. These initiatives aim to mitigate the threats and ensure that sea tortoises continue to grace our oceans for generations to come.

Evolutionary History

Sea tortoises, also known as marine turtles, boast an extensive evolutionary history that spans over 100 million years. Their journey through time is a testament to their remarkable adaptability and resilience in the face of monumental changes on Earth. These ancient reptiles trace their origins to terrestrial ancestors, from which they gradually evolved into the specialized sea dwellers we recognize today.

The evolutionary lineage of sea tortoises can be traced back to the late Jurassic period, a time when dinosaurs roamed the Earth. During this epoch, the first proto-turtles began to diverge from their land-dwelling relatives. This transition from land to sea was not a swift process but rather a gradual series of adaptations over millions of years. These adaptations included the development of flippers for swimming, streamlined bodies for efficient movement in water, and specialized salt glands for excreting excess salt consumed while living in a marine environment.

One of the most significant periods in the evolutionary timeline of sea tortoises occurred around 110 million years ago, during the Cretaceous period. This era was characterized by dramatic shifts in the Earth's climate and geography, including the breakup of the supercontinent Pangaea and the formation of vast inland seas. These environmental changes created new ecological niches and opportunities for the early ancestors of sea tortoises. In response, they evolved various physical and behavioral traits that allowed them to exploit marine habitats effectively.

Fossil records indicate that by the late Cretaceous period, sea tortoises had fully adapted to marine life. Their fossilized remains, discovered in diverse locations around the world, reveal a wide distribution and suggest that these creatures were thriving in different marine environments. This adaptability was crucial for their survival, particularly during the mass extinction event at the end of the Cretaceous period, which wiped out many other species, including the dinosaurs.

Throughout the Cenozoic era, which followed the mass extinction, sea tortoises continued to diversify and adapt. They survived multiple ice ages and periods of global warming, each time adjusting their migratory patterns, breeding behaviors, and feeding habits to cope with the changing climate. Their ability to navigate vast ocean distances and find suitable nesting sites on remote beaches has been key to their persistence through the ages.

Today, the seven extant species of sea tortoises are spread across the world's oceans, from the warm tropical waters to the cooler temperate seas. Despite the challenges they face from human activities such as habitat destruction, pollution, and climate change, sea tortoises remain a symbol of evolutionary success. Their long evolutionary history is a remarkable narrative of adaptation and endurance, showcasing the dynamic interplay between life and the ever-changing Earth.

Sea turtles are remarkable creatures that have roamed the oceans for millions of years. There are seven recognized species of sea turtles, each possessing distinct characteristics and inhabiting various marine environments. The classification of these species is primarily based on their physical traits, behaviors, and genetic differences, which help scientists and conservationists understand their unique adaptations and ecological roles.

1.   Leatherback Turtle (Dermochelys coriacea): The leatherback turtle is the largest of all sea turtle species, distinguished by its lack of a hard shell. Instead, its carapace is covered with leathery, oily flesh. These turtles are

highly migratory, traveling vast distances across oceans. They primarily feed on jellyfish and are known for their ability to dive to great depths, sometimes exceeding 1,200 meters. Leatherbacks have a broad, teardrop-shaped body and can weigh up to 2,000 pounds.

2. Green Turtle (Chelonia mydas): Named for the green color of their body fat, green turtles are primarily herbivorous, feeding on seagrasses and algae. They are often found in shallow coastal areas, bays, and estuaries. Green turtles have a smoother, more streamlined shell compared to other species and can grow up to 5 feet in length. Their populations are widely

distributed in tropical and subtropical waters around the world.

3. Loggerhead Turtle (Caretta caretta): Recognizable by their large heads and powerful jaws, loggerhead turtles are omnivorous, feeding on a variety of prey including crustaceans, mollusks, and fish. They prefer coastal habitats and are often seen near coral reefs and rocky shorelines. Loggerheads have a reddish-brown carapace and can weigh between 170 and 500 pounds. Their strong jaws enable them to crush hard-shelled prey.

4. Hawksbill Turtle (Eretmochelys imbricata): Hawksbill turtles are easily identified by their narrow, pointed beaks and beautifully patterned shells, which

are highly prized for their appearance. These turtles inhabit coral reefs and are primarily spongivores, meaning they feed mainly on sponges. Hawksbills are smaller in size compared to other sea turtles, usually weighing between 100 and 150 pounds.

5.   Olive Ridley Turtle (Lepidochelys olivacea): The olive ridley is known for its relatively small size and heart-shaped shell. They are named for the olive coloration of their carapace. Olive ridleys are omnivorous, consuming a varied diet of jellyfish, shrimp, crabs, and fish. They are famous for their mass nesting events known as "arribadas," where thousands of females come ashore to lay eggs simultaneously.

6.   Kemp's Ridley Turtle (Lepidochelys kempii): Kemp's ridley turtles are the smallest and most critically endangered of all sea turtle species. They have a similar appearance to the olive ridley but are typically lighter in color. These turtles primarily inhabit the Gulf of Mexico and the eastern seaboard of the United States. Like their relatives, they also participate in mass nesting events.

7.   Flatback Turtle (Natator depressus): Endemic to the waters of Australia, the flatback turtle has a flat, olive-gray carapace. Unlike other sea turtles, flatbacks do not migrate long distances and are usually found in shallow coastal waters, bays, and estuaries. They feed on a variety of

marine organisms including sea cucumbers, jellyfish, and soft corals.

Each of these seven sea turtle species plays a vital role in the marine ecosystem. Their diverse diets and habitats contribute to the health of ocean environments, making their conservation essential for maintaining marine biodiversity. Understanding the unique traits and behaviors of these turtles helps in creating effective conservation strategies to protect them and their habitats for future generations.

Importance In Marine Ecosystems

Sea tortoises are integral to the health and stability of marine ecosystems, playing several key roles that benefit a wide range of marine life. Their importance can be understood through their impact on seagrass beds, coral reefs, nutrient cycling, and the overall balance of marine food webs.

One of the primary ways sea tortoises contribute to marine ecosystems is through their maintenance of seagrass beds. Seagrass beds are vital habitats for many marine species, providing food, shelter, and breeding grounds. Sea tortoises graze on seagrass, preventing it from becoming overgrown and promoting the growth of healthy seagrass blades. This grazing activity enhances the productivity and biodiversity of seagrass beds. By keeping these areas healthy, sea tortoises indirectly support species such as fish, crustaceans, and mollusks that depend on seagrass habitats for survival.

In addition to their role in seagrass bed maintenance, sea tortoises also contribute significantly to the health of coral reefs. Coral reefs are some of the most diverse and productive ecosystems on the planet, but they are also fragile and susceptible to various threats. Sea tortoises help to maintain coral reefs by controlling the populations of sponges and algae that can overgrow and smother coral. For instance, hawksbill sea tortoises feed on sponges, which compete with corals for space. By keeping sponge populations in check, these tortoises allow corals to thrive, thereby supporting the myriad of species that inhabit coral reefs.

Nutrient cycling is another crucial process influenced by sea tortoises. As they consume plants and invertebrates, sea tortoises excrete waste that is rich in nutrients. These nutrients are then recycled into the ecosystem, promoting the growth of primary producers like phytoplankton and seagrass. This nutrient input is essential for maintaining the productivity of marine ecosystems, supporting food chains from the smallest microorganisms to larger predators.

Moreover, sea tortoises play a role in balancing marine food webs. They are both predators and prey within their ecosystems. As predators, they help control the populations of the species they consume, such as jellyfish, sponges, and seagrass. This predation pressure ensures that no single species dominates the ecosystem, maintaining biodiversity and ecological stability. As prey, sea tortoises provide a food source for larger marine animals, including sharks and orcas. Their presence in the food web thus supports the survival and health of these larger predators.

CHAPTER TWO

ANATOMY AND PHYSIOLOGY

Shell Structure And Function

The shell of a sea tortoise stands as its most distinguishing characteristic, fulfilling essential protective and functional roles. It consists primarily of two integral components—the carapace, which forms the upper shell, and the plastron, the lower shell. Constructed from a specialized substance called keratin, akin to the material found in human fingernails, this resilient outer layer serves as a formidable defense against predators while providing crucial structural support for the tortoise's body.

Beyond its formidable appearance, the shell is a complex structure comprised of fused bones enveloped by plates known as scutes. These scutes are not static but undergo continuous growth throughout the tortoise's life, facilitating shell expansion as the creature matures. This growth mechanism not only accommodates the tortoise's increasing size but also adapts to environmental changes and physical demands.

The variability in shape and size of the shell among different species directly impacts the tortoise's agility and buoyancy in water. Some species have evolved shells that enhance their ability to navigate aquatic environments efficiently, while others exhibit adaptations more suited to terrestrial habitats. This diversity underscores the adaptive flexibility of the tortoise shell, tailored through evolution to meet specific ecological niches and survival challenges.

Functionally, the shell serves as more than a mere protective barrier; it plays a pivotal role in thermoregulation and maintaining internal homeostasis. The shell's structure includes specialized chambers and vascular networks that help regulate body temperature and ensure metabolic efficiency, crucial for the tortoise's overall health and survival in varied habitats.

Respiratory And Circulatory Systems

Sea tortoises, known for their remarkable adaptations to marine life, possess highly specialized respiratory and circulatory systems. These adaptations allow them to thrive in aquatic environments where they spend the majority of their lives. One of the most notable features of sea tortoises is their efficient lungs, which play a crucial role in their survival. Unlike mammals that breathe continuously, sea tortoises have developed the ability to extract a significant amount of oxygen from the air they breathe at the water's surface. This capability is vital as it enables them to remain submerged for extended periods, sometimes up to several hours, while foraging for food or avoiding predators.

The respiratory system of sea tortoises is uniquely adapted to facilitate prolonged dives. Their lungs are spongy and flexible, allowing for efficient gas exchange. When a sea tortoise surfaces, it quickly fills its lungs with air. The high efficiency of their lungs ensures that a large volume of oxygen is absorbed into the bloodstream with each breath. This oxygen is then stored in their blood and muscles, providing a reserve that the tortoise can draw upon while submerged. Additionally, sea tortoises can regulate their heart rate to conserve oxygen. During a dive, their heart rate slows down significantly, reducing the amount of oxygen consumed by their body tissues and allowing them to stay underwater longer.

The circulatory system of sea tortoises, similar to other reptiles, features a three-chambered heart. This heart structure includes two atria and one ventricle. The design of the heart allows for the separation of oxygenated and deoxygenated blood, although not as completely as in mammals and birds with their four-chambered hearts. In sea tortoises, the oxygenated blood from the lungs and deoxygenated blood from the body mix to some extent within the single ventricle before being pumped throughout the body. Despite this partial mixing, the circulatory system is highly efficient in meeting the metabolic needs of the tortoise, especially during dives. Furthermore, the circulatory system of sea tortoises is adapted to support their diving behavior. When submerged, blood flow is preferentially directed to essential organs such as the brain and heart, while less critical regions receive reduced blood flow. This selective distribution ensures that vital functions are maintained even during prolonged periods without breathing. The ability to shunt blood away from certain areas helps in conserving oxygen and extending dive duration.

Digestive System And Diet

Sea tortoises exhibit remarkable adaptations in their digestive system tailored to their herbivorous diet. Their primary food sources are marine plants such as seaweed and seagrass. Unlike their terrestrial relatives, sea tortoises have evolved to efficiently process these tough, fibrous plant materials, enabling them to thrive in their aquatic environments.

The digestive system of sea tortoises begins with a beak-like mouth, which is adept at tearing and shredding marine vegetation. Once the food is ingested, it travels down the esophagus to the stomach, where the initial stages of digestion occur. The stomach of a sea tortoise is highly acidic, allowing it to break down the tough cell walls of plant material. This is a crucial adaptation, as the primary components of their diet are not only fibrous but also often covered in protective layers that require significant effort to digest.

From the stomach, the partially digested food moves into the small intestine. The small intestine is the primary site for nutrient absorption. Here, a complex interplay of enzymes and bacteria works to further break down the food into absorbable nutrients. The length and structure of the small intestine are specially adapted to maximize the extraction of nutrients from the fibrous plant material. This is a significant difference from terrestrial tortoises, which may consume a more varied diet and thus have a slightly different digestive process.

One of the most fascinating adaptations of sea tortoises is their ability to handle the salt content in their diet. Marine plants naturally contain a higher salt concentration due to their environment. To manage this, sea tortoises possess specialized salt glands, located near their eyes, which actively excrete excess salts. This adaptation prevents dehydration, a common risk for animals that ingest large amounts of saltwater or saline food. The salt glands secrete a concentrated brine that the tortoises expel, often appearing as tears, thereby maintaining their internal salt balance and hydration levels.

Additionally, the large intestine and cloaca of sea tortoises play crucial roles in the final stages of digestion and excretion. The large intestine is responsible for absorbing water and salts from the remaining indigestible food matter, which is particularly important given their saline environment. The cloaca, a multipurpose orifice, is where the final waste is expelled from the body.

These specialized digestive adaptations allow sea tortoises to thrive on a diet that would be challenging for many other animals. Their ability to efficiently process tough marine plants and manage high salt intake exemplifies the incredible evolutionary changes that have enabled them to flourish in ocean habitats. Through these adaptations, sea tortoises have become an integral part of marine ecosystems, contributing to the health and maintenance of their underwater environments.

Reproductive Anatomy And Lifecycles

Sea tortoises exhibit remarkable reproductive adaptations shaped by their marine environment. These adaptations are evident in their unique behaviors and anatomical features. One of the most notable behaviors is natal homing, where females return to the same beaches where they were born to lay their eggs. This instinctual journey can involve traveling hundreds or even thousands of miles across the ocean, guided by the Earth's magnetic field and other environmental cues.

The reproductive process begins with internal fertilization. During mating, males use their cloacas to transfer sperm into the female's cloaca. This intricate process often occurs in the water, where the turtles' buoyancy aids in positioning. The male has elongated forelimbs with claws to grip the female's shell during copulation, ensuring successful sperm transfer.

After fertilization, the female embarks on a perilous journey back to her natal beach, often navigating treacherous waters and avoiding numerous predators. Upon reaching the beach, she selects a suitable nesting site, typically above the high tide line to protect the eggs from being washed away. Using her hind flippers, she digs a deep nest in the sand, a laborious process that can take several hours. Once the nest is ready, she deposits a clutch of eggs, which can number between 50 and 200, depending on the species.

The eggs are then carefully covered with sand to camouflage them from predators and to provide insulation. The mother returns to the sea, leaving the eggs to incubate unattended. This solitary incubation period lasts about six to ten weeks, influenced by the sand's temperature. Interestingly, the temperature of the nest determines the sex of the hatchlings, with warmer temperatures typically producing females and cooler temperatures producing males.

Hatching is a critical phase in the lifecycle of sea tortoises. Emerging from their eggs, the hatchlings must dig their way to the surface, often coordinating their efforts to increase their chances of survival. Once they reach the surface, they instinctively head toward the ocean, guided by the natural light horizon over the water. This journey is fraught with dangers; hatchlings are vulnerable to predators such as birds, crabs, and other animals. Additionally, artificial lighting from coastal developments can disorient them, leading them away from the safety of the ocean.

Upon reaching the water, the young tortoises face further challenges, including predation by marine creatures and navigating ocean currents. Those that survive this critical early stage will spend several years in the open ocean before returning to coastal areas to mature and continue the cycle. The life of a sea tortoise is a testament to nature's resilience and the intricate adaptations that have evolved to ensure the survival of these ancient mariners.

CHAPTER THREE

HABITAT AND DISTRIBUTION

Global Distribution

Sea tortoises inhabit nearly every ocean across the globe, thriving in diverse marine environments from warm tropical waters to cooler temperate seas. There are seven distinct species of sea turtles, each with its own unique range and habitat preferences. Among these species, the leatherback sea turtle holds the title of the most widely distributed. This remarkable species can be found in both the Atlantic and Pacific Oceans, showcasing an impressive ability to travel vast distances between feeding grounds and nesting sites. Leatherbacks are known for their extensive migratory patterns, often crossing entire ocean basins.

Loggerhead turtles are another prevalent species, predominantly residing in the Atlantic Ocean. Their range extends along the coastlines of North and South America, Africa, and Europe. These turtles are frequently encountered in coastal regions, where they nest on sandy beaches and forage in coastal waters. Green turtles, in contrast, favor more tropical environments. Their distribution spans the warm waters of the Atlantic, Indian, and Pacific Oceans. These turtles are often associated with coral reefs, seagrass beds, and coastal lagoons, where they find abundant food sources and suitable nesting sites.

Hawksbill turtles are primarily found in tropical coral reefs, where they play a crucial role in maintaining the health of these delicate ecosystems. Their distribution includes regions in the Caribbean, the Indo-Pacific, and the western Atlantic. The critically endangered Kemp's ridley turtles have a much more restricted range, with the majority of their population concentrated in the Gulf of Mexico. These turtles are renowned for their unique nesting behavior, known as arribadas, where thousands of females come ashore simultaneously to lay their eggs on specific beaches.

Olive ridley turtles share the arribada nesting phenomenon with Kemp's ridleys, but their range is more expansive, covering tropical beaches worldwide. These synchronized mass nesting events are a spectacular sight and a vital part of the species' reproductive strategy. Lastly, the flatback turtle is the only sea turtle species confined to a relatively small geographic area. This species is endemic to the waters of Australia and Papua New Guinea, where it nests on sandy beaches and forages in shallow coastal waters.

Each sea turtle species has adapted to its environment, contributing to the rich biodiversity of our oceans. Their global distribution reflects the adaptability and resilience of these ancient mariners, but it also underscores the need for international conservation efforts to ensure their survival amid numerous threats such as habitat loss, pollution, and climate change.

Coastal And Oceanic Habitats

Sea turtles utilize a variety of habitats throughout their lives, with specific preferences often varying by species and life stage. Coastal areas, including sandy beaches, play a crucial role in their reproductive cycle. Female turtles return to these beaches, often the very ones where they were born, to lay their eggs. The sandy shores provide the necessary conditions for the eggs to incubate and hatch, ensuring the continuation of their species. The phenomenon of natal homing, where females return to their birthplace to nest, underscores the importance of protecting these critical coastal habitats.

Once the eggs hatch, the juvenile sea turtles, known as hatchlings, make their perilous journey from the nest to the ocean. This initial trek is fraught with dangers, including predators and obstacles, but reaching the water marks the beginning of their transition to oceanic habitats. Juvenile and adult sea turtles are predominantly found in different types of oceanic and coastal environments, each providing unique resources essential for their survival and growth.

Leatherback turtles, for example, are oceanic wanderers that thrive in the open ocean. They are known for their impressive diving capabilities, often reaching great depths in search of their primary food source, jellyfish. The open ocean environment provides the vast, deep waters that leatherbacks need to find sufficient food and avoid predators.

In contrast, species like the loggerhead and green turtles are more frequently associated with coastal habitats. Loggerheads often inhabit bays, estuaries, and nearshore waters where they find abundant food sources such as crustaceans and mollusks. Green turtles, named for the greenish color of their body fat resulting from their herbivorous diet, are commonly found in seagrass beds and algal-rich areas. These coastal habitats not only provide food but also offer suitable conditions for resting and avoiding predators.

Mangroves, seagrass beds, and coral reefs are particularly vital for the survival of young turtles and some adult species. Mangroves, with their dense root systems, offer protection from predators and strong currents. Seagrass beds are crucial feeding grounds for green turtles, providing the plant-based diet essential for their growth. Coral reefs, known for their biodiversity, are especially important for hawksbill turtles. The complex structures of the reefs offer both food and shelter. Hawksbills feed on sponges and other invertebrates that thrive within the reef ecosystems, making these habitats indispensable for their survival.

Migration Patterns

Sea tortoises are celebrated for their extensive migration patterns, traveling thousands of miles between feeding grounds and nesting sites. These migrations are vital for their survival and reproductive success, enabling them to access nutrient-rich feeding areas and safe nesting beaches. Among sea tortoises, the leatherback turtle stands out for undertaking one of the longest migrations of any marine animal. These turtles travel between the cold, nutrient-dense waters of the North Atlantic and the warm, tropical nesting beaches of the Caribbean.

Migration patterns of sea turtles are typically seasonal. During the colder months, they move to warmer waters to maintain their body temperature and find food. Conversely, during the breeding season, they return to specific nesting beaches. For example, loggerhead turtles in the Atlantic Ocean migrate from the coast of the United States to the waters near the Azores and Cape Verde. They follow ocean currents that not only aid their travel but also provide a plentiful supply of food.

The navigational prowess of sea turtles is a marvel of nature. Tracking studies have revealed that these creatures use a sophisticated combination of environmental cues to find their way across vast ocean distances. The Earth's magnetic field plays a significant role in their navigation. Sea turtles possess an innate ability to detect the magnetic signatures of different regions, which helps them determine their position in the ocean. This geomagnetic sense acts as a natural GPS, guiding them on their long journeys.

In addition to geomagnetic cues, sea turtles also utilize water currents to aid their navigation. These currents act as highways in the ocean, allowing the turtles to travel more efficiently and conserve energy. By riding these currents, turtles can cover great distances with less effort. For example, the Gulf Stream in the Atlantic Ocean is a well-known migratory route for many marine species, including sea turtles.

The position of the sun is another navigational tool for sea turtles. They use the angle of the sun's rays to orient themselves and maintain their direction. This solar navigation is particularly useful during long migrations when other cues might be less reliable.

The combination of these navigational strategies ensures that sea turtles can return to the same nesting beaches year after year. This fidelity to natal beaches, where they were born, is crucial for their reproductive success. By returning to these familiar sites, they can ensure the continuation of their species, as these beaches provide the optimal conditions for laying and incubating their eggs.

Environmental Adaptations

Sea tortoises have evolved a range of adaptations that enable them to thrive in diverse marine environments. Their streamlined bodies and powerful flippers are pivotal in making them efficient swimmers, capable of traveling vast distances and diving to impressive depths. For instance, leatherback turtles, distinguished by their flexible shells and large front flippers, can dive over 1,000 meters deep to hunt jellyfish.

This unique shell structure and powerful swimming capability provide them the agility and endurance needed to navigate the deep ocean.

Dietary adaptations also highlight the tortoises' specialization to their habitats. Green turtles, primarily herbivores, feed on seagrasses and algae. Their serrated jaws are specially designed to tear through tough plant material, enabling them to access and consume their preferred diet efficiently. In contrast, hawksbill turtles, which feed on sponges, have evolved narrow, pointed beaks. This adaptation allows them to extract sponges from the crevices of coral reefs, showcasing a remarkable specialization for their food sources.

Thermoregulation is another critical adaptation for sea tortoises, especially notable in leatherback turtles. Unlike other reptiles, leatherbacks can maintain a body temperature higher than the surrounding water, a phenomenon known as gigantothermy. This ability allows them to inhabit colder waters that would typically be unsuitable for other reptiles, thereby expanding their ecological range and access to different prey.

Behavioral adaptations are equally essential for their survival. Nesting females, for example, exhibit site fidelity, consistently returning to the same beaches to lay their eggs. This behavior ensures that the environmental conditions suitable for the incubation of their eggs are reliably met, increasing the likelihood of successful hatching. Such site fidelity underscores the tortoises' intricate relationship with their environment and the evolutionary importance of behavioral consistency. Additionally, sea tortoises have developed migratory patterns that align with their feeding and breeding cycles. These long-distance migrations between feeding grounds and nesting sites are crucial for their life cycle, ensuring that they can access necessary resources and suitable environments for reproduction. The ability to navigate vast oceanic distances and return to precise locations is a testament to their navigational skills, which are still not fully understood but are believed to involve a combination of geomagnetic cues and environmental landmarks.

CHAPTER FOUR

BEHAVIOR AND SOCIAL STRUCTURE

Feeding Behavior

Sea tortoises, commonly referred to as sea turtles, exhibit a diverse array of feeding behaviors that are intricately tied to their species and age. These ancient mariners have evolved to thrive on varied diets, including seagrasses, algae, jellyfish, and crustaceans. For example, the green sea turtle's diet is predominantly composed of seagrass and algae, which contribute to the greenish hue of their body fat. This dietary preference contrasts sharply with that of the leatherback sea turtle, which primarily consumes jellyfish. The leatherback's sharp, pointed jaws are specially adapted to capture and consume these gelatinous creatures effectively.

The dietary habits of sea turtles also change significantly from hatchling to adulthood. Hatchlings are omnivorous, consuming a wide variety of plant and animal matter available in the ocean. This broad diet provides them with the necessary nutrients to support rapid growth and development. As sea turtles mature, their diets become more specialized, reflecting their species-specific feeding adaptations. For instance, the beaks of sea turtles are strong and well-suited for tearing food, which is essential for consuming their preferred prey.

Sea turtles' feeding grounds are typically located in coastal areas rich in seagrasses and coral reefs. These environments provide ample food resources and are crucial for the turtles' survival. The role of feeding in sea turtles extends beyond mere sustenance; it also has significant ecological implications. Green turtles, for example, play a vital role in maintaining the health of seagrass beds. By grazing on seagrass, they prevent these beds from becoming overgrown, which helps maintain the balance of the ecosystem. Healthy seagrass beds are essential as they serve as vital habitats for numerous marine species.

Furthermore, the feeding activities of sea turtles contribute to the overall health of marine ecosystems. The grazing behavior of green turtles ensures that seagrass beds remain productive and capable of supporting a diverse array of marine life. This ecological service underscores the importance of sea turtles in marine environments, highlighting their role as keystone species that help sustain the biodiversity and functionality of their habitats.

Nesting And Reproduction

The nesting and reproductive behavior of sea turtles is an awe-inspiring natural phenomenon, showcasing the remarkable instincts and endurance of these marine creatures. One of the most fascinating aspects of this behavior is natal homing, where female sea turtles return to the very beaches where they were born to lay their eggs. This journey can span thousands of miles across the vast ocean, highlighting the turtles' incredible navigational abilities. Typically, nesting occurs at night, providing the turtles some protection from predators.

Upon reaching the beach, the female sea turtle begins the intricate and ritualized process of nesting. Using her flippers, she digs a nest in the sand. This task requires significant effort and time, often taking several hours. Once the nest is prepared, the turtle deposits a clutch of around 100 eggs. Each egg is carefully laid, and after the clutch is complete, the female meticulously covers the nest with sand. This covering serves as a protective barrier against predators and helps regulate the temperature within the nest.

The temperature of the sand plays a crucial role in the development of the eggs, particularly in determining the sex of the hatchlings. Warmer sand temperatures generally result in a higher number of female hatchlings, while cooler temperatures tend to produce more males. This temperature-dependent sex determination is a unique characteristic of sea turtles and has significant implications for their populations.

After laying and covering the eggs, the exhausted female turtle returns to the ocean. She may repeat this nesting process several times during a breeding season, but typically only once every two to three years. The eggs incubate in the sand for about two months, during which time they are vulnerable to various environmental factors and predators.

When the incubation period is over, the hatchlings begin their perilous journey to the sea. This journey, known as the "frenzy period," is guided by an instinct to move toward the brightest horizon, which is usually the ocean. However, this trek is fraught with danger. Many hatchlings fall prey to predators such as birds, crabs, and other animals. The few that survive the journey to the water face further challenges in the ocean, where they must evade aquatic predators and find food to sustain their growth.

The early life of a sea turtle is a true test of survival. Those that make it through the initial stages grow and mature in the ocean, eventually returning to their natal beaches to continue the cycle of life. This extraordinary reproductive behavior of sea turtles underscores the intricate balance and resilience of nature.

Social Interactions

Sea turtles are primarily solitary creatures, coming together mainly for mating purposes. Despite their generally solitary nature, some species display fascinating social behaviors. For instance, juvenile green sea turtles are known to congregate in "developmental habitats." These are areas abundant in food resources and offer protection from predators. By forming these groups, young turtles enhance their chances of survival through collective vigilance and social learning. This communal behavior allows juveniles to learn from each other and benefit from the increased safety that comes with being part of a group.

During the mating season, male sea turtles exhibit competitive behaviors to gain access to females. These behaviors can include physical confrontations where males use their flippers to fend off rivals. The competition among males is often intense, with stronger and more dominant males typically prevailing. These successful males then mate with females in the water, usually near the nesting beaches. This competitive aspect of mating is crucial for ensuring that the strongest genes are passed on to the next generation, thereby aiding the species' overall resilience and adaptability.

Social interactions among sea turtles are also noticeable during basking periods. Basking is a behavior where turtles rest on beaches or float at the surface of the water. This behavior is essential for thermoregulation, as basking helps turtles maintain their body temperature.

It also provides a necessary break from the energy-intensive process of foraging. While basking, sea turtles often tolerate the presence of others, showing a level of social tolerance that is not typically observed during other activities. This tolerance during basking indicates that while sea turtles are generally solitary, they can exhibit social behaviors when it is beneficial to them.

In some regions, basking behavior can be observed more frequently, and it often involves multiple turtles resting in close proximity. This behavior is particularly common in species that inhabit temperate regions, where maintaining body temperature is crucial for their metabolic processes. Basking not only aids in thermoregulation but also allows turtles to absorb UV light, which is vital for the synthesis of vitamin D, an essential nutrient for their shell health and overall well-being.

Overall, while sea turtles are predominantly solitary, their social behaviors during certain life stages and activities highlight the complexity of their interactions with each other and their environment. These behaviors, from juvenile congregation in developmental habitats to competitive mating and communal basking, illustrate the adaptive strategies that sea turtles have developed to survive and thrive in their marine habitats. The interplay of solitary and social behaviors ensures that sea turtles can effectively navigate the challenges of their environments and maintain their populations.

Communication And Navigation

Sea turtles rely on an intricate combination of sensory cues to communicate and navigate through the vast oceanic environment. Though communication among sea turtles is limited, it plays an essential role, particularly during critical periods like mating and nesting. These ancient mariners use subtle body language, such as specific head movements and flipper gestures, to signal their intentions and establish dominance within their social structures.

One of the most remarkable aspects of sea turtle behavior is their navigational ability. These creatures possess an extraordinary capacity to travel across oceans and return to their natal beaches with pinpoint accuracy. This navigational prowess is achieved through a combination of geomagnetic cues, visual landmarks, and potentially even the position of celestial bodies like the sun and stars.

Sea turtles have a magnetic sense that enables them to detect the Earth's magnetic field and use it as a natural map for orientation. This magnetic sensitivity is crucial for their long migrations and their ability to locate their birthplace after years at sea. When they are ready to nest, female sea turtles often undertake long journeys, guided by this innate magnetic compass, to return to the beaches where they were born. This remarkable homing ability ensures the continuation of their species by providing the next generation with the same favorable conditions for hatching and survival.

Scientists are still working to fully understand the complexities of the sea turtle navigation system. Studies have shown that sea turtles can detect subtle variations in the Earth's magnetic field, which they use to determine their position relative to their destination. Additionally, visual landmarks encountered during their travels might aid in their orientation and navigation. The possibility of celestial navigation, using the sun and stars as guides, is another fascinating area of research, though it is less well understood.

The intricacies of sea turtle navigation underscore the evolutionary adaptations these animals have developed over millions of years. Their ability to navigate vast distances across the open ocean and return to precise locations is a testament to the sophistication of their sensory systems. This incredible sense of direction not only highlights the evolutionary ingenuity of sea turtles but also emphasizes the importance of preserving their natural habitats. Protecting the nesting sites and migratory pathways of sea turtles is vital for ensuring their continued survival and the perpetuation of these master navigators in the marine environment.

CHAPTER FIVE

CONSERVATION AND THREATS

Human Impact And Pollution

Human activities have a profound and often detrimental impact on sea tortoises, with pollution being one of the most significant threats. The pervasive presence of plastics in the oceans poses a severe risk to these ancient mariners. Sea tortoises frequently mistake floating plastic bags for jellyfish, a common component of their diet. Ingesting these plastic items can be fatal, leading to blockages in their digestive systems and often resulting in death. This ingestion issue is exacerbated by the sheer volume of plastic debris in the ocean, stemming from improper waste disposal and inadequate waste management practices globally.

Oil spills are another major pollutant that endangers sea tortoises. When oil contaminates the ocean, it coats the surface of the water and the shorelines, affecting the entire marine ecosystem. Sea tortoises exposed to oil suffer from skin irritation, respiratory problems, and a compromised immune system, making them more susceptible to diseases. The toxic components of oil can also poison these animals if ingested.

Chemical pollution, including pesticides, heavy metals, and other toxic substances, further exacerbates the challenges faced by sea tortoises. These chemicals enter the ocean through agricultural runoff, industrial discharges, and urban runoff. Once in the ocean, they can accumulate in the tissues of sea tortoises, leading to long-term health issues and reproductive problems. The bioaccumulation of these toxins in the food chain means that even trace amounts can have devastating effects over time.

Discarded fishing gear, such as nets and lines, poses a significant entanglement hazard for sea tortoises. These creatures can become ensnared in this debris, leading to injuries, impaired movement, or drowning. The proliferation of ghost fishing gear, which continues to catch and kill marine life long after being abandoned, further compounds this problem. Efforts to retrieve and properly dispose of abandoned fishing gear are critical in mitigating this threat.

Coastal development is another human activity that adversely affects sea tortoises, particularly their nesting sites. As coastal areas are developed for tourism, housing, and industry, the natural habitats of sea tortoises are destroyed or severely altered. This habitat loss leads to a decline in suitable nesting sites, reducing the number of hatchlings that can successfully reach the ocean. Additionally, beachfront lighting from properties can disorient hatchlings. Newly emerged sea tortoise hatchlings instinctively move towards the brightest horizon, typically the moonlight reflecting off the ocean. Artificial lights from beachfront developments can lead them astray, directing them inland where they face a myriad of dangers, including predation, dehydration, and traffic.

Climate Change Effects

Climate change presents a profound and escalating threat to sea tortoises, impacting their habitats and reproductive patterns in significant ways. One of the most critical issues stems from rising temperatures, which directly influence the sand temperature where sea tortoises lay their eggs. This is pivotal because the sex of hatchlings is determined by the temperature of the sand during incubation. Warmer sands lead to a higher proportion of female hatchlings, skewing the natural sex ratio. This imbalance poses a serious concern for the future sustainability of sea tortoise populations, as it can disrupt breeding dynamics and genetic diversity.

In addition to altering sex ratios, climate change also exacerbates coastal erosion, which directly affects nesting beaches essential for sea tortoises. Rising sea levels and more frequent and intense storms contribute to the erosion of these beaches, diminishing the available area for nesting. This reduction in suitable nesting sites further compounds the challenges sea tortoises face in successfully reproducing and perpetuating their species.

Beyond nesting grounds, warmer ocean temperatures driven by climate change have broader ecological repercussions for sea tortoises. These rising temperatures can disrupt the distribution and availability of the tortoises' prey species, such as sea grasses and algae. As these primary food sources shift or decline in abundance, sea tortoises may be forced to travel longer distances in search of sustenance. Such disruptions to their feeding patterns can lead to decreased fitness and reproductive success, impacting population health over time.

Moreover, the overall resilience of sea tortoises to climate stressors is further compromised by their slow growth rates and delayed sexual maturity. These biological characteristics make them particularly vulnerable to rapid environmental changes, such as those induced by climate change, which outpace their adaptive capacities.

Efforts to mitigate these impacts involve both conservation measures and broader climate change mitigation strategies. Protecting and restoring nesting habitats, implementing measures to reduce coastal erosion, and monitoring and managing marine ecosystems are crucial steps. Additionally, global efforts to curb greenhouse gas emissions and address climate change on a systemic level are imperative to safeguarding the long-term survival of sea tortoises and their ecosystems.

Conservation Efforts And Legislation

Conservation efforts play a pivotal role in safeguarding the survival of sea tortoises, vital to the delicate marine ecosystems they inhabit. International agreements, most notably the Convention on International Trade in Endangered Species (CITES), are instrumental in regulating the trade of tortoise products. These measures help mitigate exploitation pressures by imposing strict controls on international trade and ensuring that sea tortoises are not subjected to unsustainable harvesting practices.

At the national level, numerous countries have enacted stringent laws to protect sea tortoises and their eggs. These laws often include bans on hunting and trading sea tortoises, creating a legal framework aimed at reducing direct threats to their populations. Additionally, the establishment of protected areas such as marine reserves and national parks plays a crucial role. These designated zones provide safe havens where sea tortoises can nest, breed, and forage without the looming threat of human interference. By safeguarding these habitats, authorities aim to mitigate habitat loss and disturbance, thereby promoting population recovery.

Community-based conservation initiatives further bolster these efforts by engaging local communities in conservation activities. These programs often focus on educating local populations about the importance of sea tortoises and their habitats. By fostering a sense of stewardship among residents, these initiatives encourage sustainable practices and discourage harmful activities that could jeopardize tortoise populations. Moreover, involving local communities in monitoring and protecting nesting sites enhances conservation effectiveness, as community members become active participants in preserving critical habitats.

Education plays a pivotal role in these conservation strategies, raising awareness about the plight of sea tortoises and the broader implications of their decline. Through outreach and educational campaigns, conservationists seek to cultivate a deeper understanding of the ecological roles played by sea tortoises and the interconnectedness of marine ecosystems. By empowering individuals with knowledge, these efforts aim to foster long-term commitment to conservation principles and practices.

Rehabilitation And Rescue Programs

Rehabilitation and rescue programs are crucial for the survival of sea tortoises, playing a pivotal role in their conservation efforts worldwide. These initiatives are dedicated to rescuing and rehabilitating injured or sick sea tortoises, which often fall victim to human activities such as pollution and accidental entanglement in fishing gear.

The primary objective of these programs is to provide essential medical treatment and care to these distressed animals. When a sea tortoise is found injured or ill, whether due to ingesting plastic debris or sustaining injuries from fishing nets, dedicated teams from rehabilitation centers step in. These centers are equipped with veterinary expertise and facilities designed to handle the specific needs of sea tortoises. The initial phase involves assessing the extent of injuries or illnesses and administering appropriate medical interventions. This may include removing foreign objects like plastic or treating wounds caused by entanglement.

Once stabilized, the rehabilitation process focuses on nursing the sea tortoise back to health. This phase is critical and can vary in length depending on the severity of the initial condition. Rehabilitation centers provide a controlled environment where the tortoise can recover without further exposure to hazards present in the wild. This includes ensuring proper nutrition, monitoring health indicators, and allowing the tortoise to regain strength and mobility.

Throughout the rehabilitation period, caretakers also work on minimizing stress for the tortoise, which can significantly impact recovery. This may involve minimizing human interaction to prevent undue stress and providing enrichment activities to stimulate natural behaviors. Rehabilitation centers often collaborate with research institutions to gather data on the rehabilitation process, which helps improve treatment protocols and conservation strategies.

Public awareness campaigns are another integral component of these programs. These initiatives aim to educate communities about the threats faced by sea tortoises and how human activities contribute to their decline. Key messages include advocating for responsible waste disposal to reduce plastic pollution, promoting sustainable fishing practices to minimize accidental bycatch, and encouraging beachgoers to respect sea turtle nesting habitats.

By engaging local communities and stakeholders through education and outreach, these campaigns foster a sense of responsibility and stewardship towards sea tortoises and their habitats. They highlight the interconnectedness of human actions and the well-being of marine ecosystems, emphasizing the role each individual can play in conservation efforts.

Monitoring and tracking rehabilitated sea tortoises post-release is another critical aspect of these programs. This phase involves using satellite tracking or other methods to monitor the movements and behavior of rehabilitated individuals once they are returned to the wild. Gathering data on their survival rates, migration patterns, and habitat preferences provides valuable insights for conservationists. This information helps refine rehabilitation techniques and inform broader conservation strategies aimed at protecting sea tortoises in their natural environment.

CHAPTER SIX

RESEARCH AND TECHNOLOGICAL ADVANCES

Tracking And Monitoring Techniques

Tracking and monitoring techniques for sea tortoises have undergone remarkable evolution thanks to technological advancements. Initially, researchers primarily utilized basic tagging methods to gain insights into these creatures' movements and behaviors. However, with the advent of sophisticated technologies such as satellite telemetry and GPS tracking, our ability to gather precise data has been transformed. These modern techniques now provide detailed information on crucial aspects like migration patterns, feeding grounds, and habitat utilization. In the past, basic tagging involved attaching identification tags to sea tortoises, allowing researchers to track their movements over time. While informative, this method was limited in its scope and often provided only intermittent data points. The introduction of satellite telemetry revolutionized the field by enabling real-time tracking over vast oceanic expanses. This technology works by fitting individual tortoises with transmitters that communicate location data via satellites, offering continuous monitoring without the limitations of traditional methods.

GPS tracking further enhances our understanding by pinpointing exact locations of sea tortoises with unprecedented accuracy. Researchers can now map out detailed migration routes, identify specific feeding areas, and determine the spatial extent of their habitat use. This level of detail is crucial for conservation efforts, as it allows scientists to pinpoint critical areas where sea tortoises congregate or traverse during different phases of their life cycle.

Moreover, these advanced techniques not only track individual tortoises but also contribute invaluable data for broader conservation strategies. By identifying key habitats and migration corridors, conservationists can prioritize protection measures in areas most crucial for the species' survival. This proactive approach is essential given the ongoing threats sea tortoises face from habitat loss, pollution, climate change, and incidental capture in fisheries.

Genetic Studies

Genetic studies are fundamental in unraveling the intricate details of sea tortoises, shedding light on their population structure, evolutionary trajectory, and genetic diversity. Through advanced DNA analysis, researchers can discern distinct populations, evaluate their genetic robustness, and explore their adaptive capacities amidst changing environments. This profound understanding plays a pivotal role in formulating targeted conservation initiatives aimed at safeguarding these iconic creatures.

Sea tortoises, encompassing various species like the loggerhead, green, and leatherback, face numerous threats ranging from habitat loss to climate change. Genetic studies provide a crucial toolset for scientists to navigate these challenges. By examining genetic markers across populations, researchers can delineate different genetic lineages and pinpoint regions of high genetic diversity. Such insights not only highlight key hotspots for conservation but also reveal potential corridors for genetic exchange crucial for maintaining healthy population dynamics.

Moreover, genetic analyses unearth the evolutionary history of sea tortoises, elucidating how past environmental shifts have shaped their genetic makeup. This historical perspective is invaluable in predicting their resilience to contemporary environmental pressures and forecasting future adaptation potentials. For instance, studying genetic adaptations in response to varying ocean temperatures can inform strategies to mitigate the impacts of climate change on these vulnerable species.

Equally significant is the role of genetic studies in addressing genetic bottlenecks—periods of reduced genetic diversity that threaten the long-term viability of populations. By identifying populations with limited genetic variation, conservationists can prioritize efforts to bolster genetic resilience through targeted breeding programs or habitat restoration initiatives. This proactive approach aims to mitigate the risk of inbreeding depression and increase the adaptive potential of sea tortoises facing uncertain ecological futures.

Impact Of Research On Conservation

Research on sea tortoises plays a pivotal role in shaping conservation strategies and policies, leveraging scientific evidence to guide effective management and protective measures. By focusing on key aspects such as habitat degradation, bycatch mitigation, and climate change impacts, scientific studies underscore the critical need for proactive conservation efforts.

Habitat degradation remains a significant threat to sea tortoises, driven by coastal development, pollution, and alteration of nesting beaches. Research illuminates the specific impacts of these factors on nesting sites and foraging grounds, emphasizing the urgency of habitat preservation and restoration initiatives. By pinpointing vulnerable areas and understanding the ecological requirements of sea tortoises, researchers inform targeted conservation actions aimed at maintaining essential habitats.

Bycatch, the incidental capture of sea tortoises in fishing gear, poses another major threat highlighted through research. Studies quantify bycatch rates, identify high-risk areas, and evaluate gear modifications and fishing practices to reduce unintentional harm. These findings support the development and implementation of bycatch mitigation strategies, including the use of turtle excluder devices (TEDs) in fishing nets and spatial-temporal fishing restrictions in critical habitats. Effective mitigation measures informed by research are crucial in minimizing sea tortoise mortality and preserving population stability.

Furthermore, research underscores the profound impacts of climate change on sea tortoises, including rising sea temperatures, altered ocean currents, and sea-level rise. These factors disrupt nesting behaviors, affect food availability, and increase susceptibility to diseases, compounding existing threats. Scientific investigations into climate change impacts enable adaptive management responses, such as establishing resilient marine protected areas, promoting sustainable fisheries practices, and engaging local communities in conservation efforts.

Conservation initiatives rooted in scientific research aim not only to mitigate immediate threats but also to foster long-term resilience and sustainability. Collaborative efforts between researchers, policymakers, conservation organizations, and local communities are essential for translating research findings into actionable policies and practices. These initiatives seek to restore sea tortoise populations, safeguard critical habitats, and promote sustainable livelihoods that coexist harmoniously with marine ecosystems.

Future Directions In Sea Tortoise Research

Looking forward, the trajectory of sea tortoise research is set to tackle pressing challenges and explore unresolved inquiries. The field is increasingly focused on understanding how climate change impacts nesting habitats, seeking to mitigate its effects through proactive conservation measures. One pivotal avenue of investigation involves advancing non-invasive monitoring techniques to better track population dynamics and health trends without disturbing natural behaviors.

Another crucial frontier lies in the exploration of innovative conservation strategies, including the application of assisted reproductive technologies

(ART). These technologies offer promising avenues for bolstering population numbers and genetic diversity in endangered sea tortoise species. By harnessing ART, researchers aim to mitigate the impact of habitat loss, pollution, and other anthropogenic pressures threatening these iconic reptiles.

The future of sea tortoise research hinges on collaborative efforts spanning disciplines and international borders. Such partnerships are essential for pooling resources, expertise, and data across diverse research initiatives. By fostering synergies between scientists, conservationists, and policymakers, these collaborations can drive comprehensive conservation strategies that address multifaceted challenges facing sea tortoises.

In addition to technological advancements, future research will delve deeper into the behavioral ecology of sea tortoises. Understanding their foraging habits, migration patterns, and social dynamics is crucial for informing effective conservation strategies. Furthermore, ongoing studies seek to unravel the complexities of disease ecology within sea tortoise populations, identifying threats and developing mitigation strategies to safeguard their health.

Education and public engagement are also pivotal in the conservation of sea tortoises. Increasing awareness about the ecological importance of these species and the threats they face can inspire collective action and support for conservation efforts. Outreach initiatives that involve local communities and stakeholders are integral to fostering stewardship and sustainable practices that benefit both sea tortoises and their habitats.

Looking ahead, the field of sea tortoise research is poised for continued innovation and collaboration. By addressing emerging challenges and leveraging cutting-edge technologies, researchers strive to ensure a future where sea tortoises thrive in their natural habitats, enriching marine ecosystems for generations to come.

CHAPTER SEVEN

CULTURAL AND ECONOMIC SIGNIFICANCE

Sea Tortoises In Mythology And Folklore

Sea tortoises have held a timeless fascination in human culture, featuring prominently in mythology and folklore across diverse civilizations. These majestic creatures symbolize enduring themes of longevity, wisdom, and resilience, embedding themselves deeply in the collective imagination worldwide.

In Hawaiian mythology, the green sea turtle assumes a revered role as the "aumakua," a guardian spirit believed to protect families and guide ancestral souls. This spiritual significance underscores its esteemed place in

Hawaiian culture, where it embodies a profound connection between humans and the natural world.

Similarly, within Indigenous Australian Dreamtime narratives, the turtle emerges as a pivotal figure in creation myths. Here, it symbolizes spiritual links to both land and sea, weaving intricate tales that emphasize its role in shaping the landscape and fostering ecological balance. These stories reflect a deep reverence for the turtle's intrinsic value beyond its physical presence, highlighting its significance as a cultural icon and a testament to the interdependence of all living beings.

Beyond mythology, sea tortoises serve as keystone species in marine ecosystems, playing critical roles in maintaining biodiversity and ecological health. Their habitats in coastal waters and nesting sites are integral to the stability of coastal ecosystems, influencing the dynamics of marine life and the health of coral reefs. As herbivores, they help regulate seagrass beds, which are vital nurseries for numerous marine species, thereby contributing to the overall resilience of marine habitats against environmental stressors.

Throughout history, human societies have drawn inspiration from the sea tortoise's majestic form and enduring presence. Whether as a symbol of spiritual guidance, ecological stewardship, or cultural heritage, these ancient creatures continue to captivate imaginations and underscore the intrinsic connections between humanity and the natural world. Their stories in folklore and mythology serve as timeless reminders of our intertwined destinies and the imperative to protect these gentle giants for generations to come.

Ecotourism And Economic Impact

Sea tortoises play a pivotal role in ecotourism, attracting numerous tourists to coastal regions worldwide. These ancient creatures captivate visitors with their majestic presence and unique behaviors, forming the cornerstone of sustainable tourism initiatives in countries such as the Maldives, Costa Rica, and Australia. The economic impact of sea tortoise tourism extends far beyond mere fascination, deeply influencing local economies and conservation efforts alike.

In destinations like the Maldives, where pristine marine habitats are home to diverse sea tortoise species, tourism revolving around these gentle giants has flourished. Tourists eagerly embark on guided tours and wildlife viewing expeditions, seeking glimpses of tortoises gracefully navigating their oceanic habitats. These experiences not only enrich travelers but also generate significant revenue for local communities. Revenue streams from ecotourism bolster livelihoods through employment in tour operations, hospitality services, and conservation projects.

Costa Rica presents another compelling example of how sea tortoise tourism supports sustainable development. The country's commitment to conservation has intertwined with tourism initiatives, promoting responsible wildlife encounters and environmental education. Visitors contribute directly to conservation efforts through participation in beach patrols, nesting site monitoring, and educational programs focused on marine biodiversity. This interactive approach not only raises awareness but also fosters a sense of stewardship among tourists, encouraging them to support ongoing conservation endeavors financially and through advocacy.

Australia, with its iconic Great Barrier Reef and nesting sites for species like the green and loggerhead turtles, illustrates the profound economic value of sea tortoise ecotourism. Local economies benefit from guided tours that showcase turtle nesting and hatchling releases, attracting eco-conscious travelers eager to contribute to conservation while enjoying unparalleled natural beauty. These experiences are crucial for sustaining local livelihoods dependent on marine tourism and conserving fragile ecosystems threatened by climate change and human activities.

The economic significance of sea tortoise tourism underscores the imperative of preserving healthy populations and habitats. Sustainable tourism practices ensure that future generations can continue to appreciate and derive economic benefits from these ancient marine creatures. By promoting conservation-minded tourism policies and fostering community engagement, coastal nations can harness the economic potential of sea tortoises while safeguarding their natural environments for years to come. Thus, sea tortoise ecotourism serves as a beacon of how tourism can harmoniously coexist with conservation, benefiting both local communities and global biodiversity efforts.

Educational And Awareness Campaigns

Educational campaigns are pivotal in the ongoing efforts to heighten awareness and promote conservation of sea tortoises. These initiatives are a collaborative endeavor involving schools, conservation organizations, and governmental bodies, united in their mission to educate communities about the numerous threats facing sea tortoises. These threats include habitat loss due to coastal development, pollution from marine debris and oil spills, and the illegal trade in tortoise products.

The core objective of these educational endeavors is to foster a deeper understanding of these challenges among the public. This is achieved through a variety of outreach strategies that aim to engage and empower individuals to become proactive stewards of marine conservation. Central to these efforts are interactive workshops that provide hands-on learning experiences, educational materials such as pamphlets and videos that disseminate crucial information, and organized field trips that allow participants to witness firsthand the habitats and challenges faced by sea tortoises.

Schools play a pivotal role in these campaigns by integrating conservation education into their curricula, ensuring that young learners are equipped with the knowledge and motivation to safeguard marine ecosystems. Conservation organizations often lead these educational initiatives, leveraging their expertise to develop scientifically accurate and compelling content. Governments provide essential support through policy frameworks and funding, enabling the scalability and sustainability of these educational programs.

By enhancing environmental literacy and fostering a sense of stewardship, these campaigns empower communities to take tangible actions in support of sea tortoise conservation. This might involve advocating for stronger environmental protections, participating in beach clean-ups to mitigate pollution, or supporting local conservation efforts financially or through volunteer work. The ultimate goal is to cultivate a collective commitment to preserving sea tortoises and their habitats for future generations.

Role In Sustainable Marine Practices

Sea tortoises are integral to promoting sustainable marine practices through their vital ecological roles. As herbivores, these creatures contribute significantly to the health and balance of marine ecosystems, particularly seagrass beds and coral reefs. Their primary function lies in grazing on algae, which helps prevent overgrowth that could otherwise smother these critical habitats. This grazing behavior not only maintains the structural integrity of seagrass beds and coral reefs but also fosters conditions conducive to diverse marine life.

Conservation strategies focused on sea tortoises often revolve around the establishment of marine protected areas (MPAs) and the promotion of sustainable fishing practices. These measures aim to safeguard the habitats essential for sea tortoises while also supporting broader ecosystem health.

By designating MPAs, authorities can create zones where human activities are regulated to minimize disturbances to tortoise habitats. This approach not only protects tortoises directly but also helps preserve the overall biodiversity and resilience of marine environments.

Integrating sea tortoise conservation into marine management plans is crucial for mitigating anthropogenic impacts on marine ecosystems. Such efforts involve collaboration among stakeholders including governments, conservation organizations, scientists, and local communities. By collectively working towards sustainable practices and habitat protection, these stakeholders can ensure the long-term survival of sea tortoises and the ecological benefits they provide.

Furthermore, the resilience of marine ecosystems is enhanced through the presence of sea tortoises. Their grazing habits help maintain the balance between algae and other marine flora, thereby supporting a healthy food web and ecosystem dynamics. This balance is particularly critical in regions where human activities, such as overfishing or pollution, threaten marine biodiversity.

THE END